My mission in life is not merely to survive, but to thrive; and to do so with some passion, some compassion, some humor, and some style.

Maya Angelou

Introduction

I was a Realtor for over 14 years and have been a Mortgage Broker since 1999. I have assisted many investors in finding properties to invest in and make huge profits and one day I realized that I could be doing it for myself, so I decided to jump in and start flipping houses. I bought books, watched videos attended seminars and webinars about flipping property. I learned a great deal about projecting profits, marketing the properties, however not one book talked about the day to day process of a flip. Well no one prepared me for the headaches involved in day to day process of the renovation of a property. With that in mind I decided to put together a book to share my experiences and everything I learned during the process of my flip.

When I started trying to do flips, I found myself being very frustrated because I bought into the idea that I did not need any money to purchase the property as I was told this by so many "experts". I quickly found out that I needed money for Ernest money, appraisal, down payment, and closing costs. I tried to get a loan from my bank, private investors but nothing worked. I contacted one lender that assured me all I needed was $4300.00 but, in the end, they required me to come to the table with about $30,000.00. It was a very frustrating time, as I had learned from all the books webinars, seminars online courses that I could get into the business without using my own money. I had nearly given up on the idea of flipping property when a friend approached me about working together so I partnered with her and we started working.

As my frustration grew, I found myself wanting to give up, so my goal is to give you valuable information about securing the financing, finding the property, setting a realistic budget and the actual rehab. So, in this book I want to share with you my experiences with my projects, the obstacles I have encountered, mistakes I made but most importantly how to avoid those mistakes and have a successful smooth transaction.

TYPES FINANCING

One of the first steps you need to take when considering Fix & Flips is what type of financing you will be using. There are three major financing options for funding your real estate investment deal. Traditional investor loans, Private lending and Hard money lending. Before you chose, make sure you understand each option and research the lenders for the best terms and conditions for you to have a successful flip.

1. Traditional investor loans
   a. minimum credit score, usually 680
   b. Minimum Down Payment 20-30%
   c. Do not finance the rehab
   d. 2 years min experience if you are holding the property for rental income.

2. Private lending
   a. Flexible qualification requirements
   b. Short Term Loan
   c. Higher Interest rates
   d. Interest only payments
   e. LTV depends on lender requirement
   f. May finance rehab costs

3. Hard money loans
   a. ARV based
   b. Higher interest rates
   c. Min Down Payment 10%
   d. Will finance Rehab on a Draw basis
   e. Short term
   f. Typically, no min. credit score
   g. LTV 70 to 85% of ARV

I personally have used Hard Money for my flips. Here's what I learned. Hard money lenders do not approve based on your credit for the most part, but they do look at your credit. So, they will pull your credit, if you are sensitive about your credit being pulled, prepare for that. The approval will be based mostly on the property however if you have bankruptcies, judgments and other major credit issues, that may prevent you from being able to qualify. Next, most lenders will not go out and look at the property before the deal is under contract. They work with the numbers you provide and will require an appraisal. Make sure that you are being objective when calculating the ARV (After Repair Value) of the property, avoid wasting $600-$700 on an appraisal only to find out that your numbers were completely off. So, have your agent do a CMA and find some real comps, befriend an appraiser and pick their brain about how to figure out that ARV. When presenting the deal to your lender they will ask you for a Scope of work, this is the form in which you will give the lender detailed information about the project and the costs for each and everything you will be renovating and or replacing. When you walk the property with your contractor be specific as to what work is to be performed and include this information in the Scope of Work sheet. When you submit your scope of work to the lender, be very specific as to what you will be doing to the property, do a line by line detailed breakdown of cost of labor and type of materials for each item in the renovation. The lender will provide this scope of work to the appraiser and based on that scope of work the appraiser will stablish the ARV in comparison to other properties within the area. If possible, meet the appraiser at the property so you can share with him your vision of what will be done to the property. If you have 3d models of the design, provide that to the lender as well. This will help them see your vision better and help you get that needed ARV.

Chose the loan that best fits your needs. Remember you will always need some out of pocket money so plan accordingly. When you look at a property figure out the out of pocket investment per the loan type you will use. For example:

Hard Money: Sales Price $60,000.00 down Payment:(10%) $6,000.00

Points/Closing costs: $5,000.00+ Total: $11,000.00 Cash to close

FINDING THE PROPERTY

How are you looking for your properties, how will you know if it is a good investment? There are many different ways to find investment properties. Below are a few I have used.

1. Team up with a real estate agent.
    - Interview a few and pick their brain about their knowledge of the market area and contract negotiation.
    - It is very important that your agent knows what you are trying to do,
    - and that the agent is well versed or at least willing to learn about your market area.
    - An agent will be able to give you an opinion on value before you submit offers.

2. Purchase the Pre-Foreclosure
    - Review the properties that are coming up for sale
    - Do the CMA to establish value
    - Visit the neighborhood
    - Knock on doors
    - Start negotiations with the current owner to purchase prior to the foreclosure.

3. Another source for potential investment properties is the actual foreclosure auction.
    - Get the foreclosure list form your county
    - review the market values vs the amounts owed on these properties,
    - get your proof of funds (POF) from your lender and get to that auction.
    - Keep in mind that you most likely will not be able to tour the property until you own it.

4. You can also just hunt down some for sale by owner (FSBO) properties. Just make sure you do your research on the market.

5. Reach out to local Wholesalers

- Get on their buyer list
- Have them send you potential properties
- Always do your due diligence when it comes to property values
- Tour the property with your contractor for rehab estimates

I personally work with an agent that actively looks for properties, does the CMAs before bringing the property to me. So, when she brings a property all I do is asses the rehab and budget. Not having to chase properties myself saves me a lot of time. I focus on getting the quotes from the contractors and working the numbers to present to the lender.

You can search for properties yourself, but I recommend always getting a CMA done before you even get quotes from contractors. The lender will require that an appraisal is done before funding the deal, so you want to make sure that your get as close to the ARV as possible to avoid headaches and wasted money. If you have access to MLS you can pull up the recent sales in the area, the current listed properties and compare those to your property to predict the price of your property once you complete the rehab. The easiest way to get this step done, is to have your agent assist with the CMA at least until you gain enough knowledge and experience gathering and comparing comps for your property. You can still do a CMA even if you personally do not have access to MLS. You can go on Realtor.com or HAR and look at active properties, you can also find out the recent sales in the area and compare prices for your property.

15815 Mill Hollow Drive
Houston, TX 77084

Sold Comparable Properties

Address	Subdivision	BR	Bths	#Gar	Stories	Pool	Lotsize	Year Built	Sqft.	Sold Date	Sold $	SP/SF	List $	LP/SF
15815 Mill Hollow Drive	Bear Creek Village	3	2	2	1	No	8,625	1975	1,826				$109,900	60.19
15611 Tumbling Rapids	Bear Creek Village Sec 06	3	2	2	1	No	8,378	1977	1,754	06/19/2018	$185,000	$105.47	$198,900	$113.40
4518 Hickory Downs	Bear Creek Village Sec 09	3	2	2	1	No	6,168	1977	1,887	05/22/2018	$175,000	$92.74	$185,900	$98.52
15634 Pagehurst	Bear Creek Village	3	2	2	1	No	6,720	1980	1,743	06/01/2018	$165,000	$94.66	$172,000	$98.68
15610 Pine Mountain	Bear Creek Village Sec 06	3	2	2	1	No	8,395	1977	1,842	07/02/2018	$183,000	$99.35	$182,500	$99.08
5014 Stanhope	Bear Creek Village Sec 02 R/P	3	2	2	1	No	7,475	1974	1,774	06/15/2018	$170,000	$95.83	$169,900	$95.77
15827 Echo Canyon	Bear Creek Village Sec 07	3	2	2	1	No	7,664	1977	1,628	07/20/2018	$170,000	$104.42	$165,000	$101.35

THE REHAB BUDGET

You have now identified the property you want to place a bid on. Now you need to figure out how much money you need to rehab the property and add value. Tour the property and take lots and lots of notes on the property. What type of repairs it needs, what type of changes do you want to make to the property? Do research on the materials you will use, such as Tile, Granite, Drywall, paint etc. Have an idea of how much these cost so that you can budget yourself. Do research on labor, there are plenty of websites providing local and national averages for the cost of labor. This will give you a ball park idea of how much money you will need for your rehab. With this info in hand, get with a contractor, interview several contractors before deciding who you will work with, get several bids on the scope of work you'd like to do to the property. Have everything in writing when you tour the property with the contractors, make sure to give detailed descriptions of the scope of work so that the contractors can give you detailed bids for the work and materials. For you to negotiate pricing effectively, you must have an idea of how much market rate is for the work you need completed.

It is very important that you have written detailed quotes so that you know how much money you will need for each project within the property. Once you have your quotes compare them and run the numbers. Which is the most reasonable quote, (not necessarily the cheapest). Keep in mind that the cheapest quote may not  necessarily be the most reasonable. Cheap may turn out to be expensive in the long run.

With your quote in hand you can now see how much money you will need to invest in order to make a profit. Let's do a quick exercise to figure out profits:

Property as is sales price:	**$70,000.00**
Rehab:	**$30,000.00**
Total Investment	**$100,000.00**
ARV	**$160,000.00**
Loan Amount	**$100,000.00**
Down Payment	**$7,000.00**
CC for purchase	**$4,000.00**
R.E. Comm.	**$9,600.00**
Sale CC	**$6,400.00**
Mortgage Payments	**$4,500.00**
Potential Profit:	**$28,500.00**

How did I come up with $28,500.00? Well Here is the simple formula. Keep in mind these numbers work only if your sale your property at After Repair Value (ARV). Real Estate commission has been calculated at 6% for this example. You can always negotiate other terms with your agent. Closing costs were calculated at 4% for the purchase and 4% on the sale, these also vary.

Take the ARV or sales price $160,000.00 Subtract total investment: Purchase amount + Rehab + Down Payment+ Closing Costs+ Real Estate Comm + mortgage payments = $131,500.00 This was your total investment. $160,000.00 - $131,500.00 = $28,500.00

Keep in mind that not all investments will yield the same profits this is just an example. Always set aside 20-30% cushion on your rehab budget for unexpected expenses. So, if your contractor says $30,000.00 you should have an additional $6,000.00-$9,000.00 set aside just in case.

Looking at the example above you can see that you have plenty of room in the budget to cover the 30k + cushion and make a profit. But let's say that the appraisal comes in lower than what you expected, then what? What is the least amount you need/want to make? Knowing your bottom line will keep you grounded and  pleasantly surprised if you exceed that amount. So, for the sake of the exercise let's say that your bottom line is $15,000.00. What is the lowest ARV you can get from the appraiser to net that amount of money? Always figure out your top dollar and your bottom line! If your bottom-line profit is 15k, your lowest ARV must be 145k. Remember to set realistic goals for your profit margins. Not all properties yield the same profits and every flip is different.

There are tools in Excel you can use to calculate your budget. Use excel to create formulas to figure out your profits, your expenses. If you go with a Hard Money loan, the lender will provide you with a Scope of Work form for you to input the detailed costs of the rehab. I have created an easy, plug and play spreadsheet to help me figure out my profits. See it below and get a free copy at: https://www.pattyporto.com/ebooks

I work with several hard money lenders, they provided me with closing costs scenarios prior to submitting an offer to purchase the property. This  allows me to know about how much money I would need for closing, aside from my down payment. I usually create a Comparative market Analysis (CMA) for the property I'm looking at, I do a rough estimate on the cost of the rehab and give those numbers to my lender. Once my representative receives my transaction detail, he sends me a closing cost scenario and a Proof of Funds (POF) letter. Once I have the POF and the numbers make sense, I submit my contract offer.

Below are two examples for budget tracking sheets, one I found on excel to help me track my budget, it consists of two pages and it shows me when I am over my budget which is super helpful. Sometimes we can get carried away buying things or paying for labor that was not in the initial quote and before we know it, we are cutting into our profits. This form helps keep me grounded. The second form is from a lender, it's their "Scope of Work from" This form gives the lender detail of the rehab costs. Make sure that you give as much detail as possible in your scope of work sheet. Always keep in mind that the lender will give the appraiser the scope of work form and the appraiser will give their opinion on value based on the amount of work and the types of materials you will be using during your rehab. So be specific!

FLIP PROFIT CALCULATOR

ACQUISITION COSTS

						AMOUNT
PURCHASE PRICE					$	120,000.00
CLOSING COSTS				4%	$	4,000.00
DOWN PAYMENT				10%	$	10,000.00
REHAB AMOUNT					$	30,000.00
OTHER EXPENSES						
TOTAL INVESTMENT					**$ 144,000.00**	

ARV	**$ 180,000.00**
SALES PRICE	**$ 175,000.00**

SALES COSTS

R.E. COMM				6%	$	10,500.00
CLOSING COSTS				4%	$	7,000.00
OTHER EXPENSES						
TOTAL COST TO SALE					**$ 17,500.00**	

PROFIT	**$ 13,500.00**

Sample Rehab Budget from Excel

HOME CONSTRUCTION BUDGET

PROJECT INFORMATION

Project Name	
Project Description	New Kitchen, Master Bath, 2nd Bath, Sheetrock entire house, Replace 30 2x4s in frame, Paint, cosmetic finishes
Contractor	
Contact Name	
Phone	
Address	

FINANCIAL STATUS

Cash Amount	$0
Financed Amount	$30,000
Total Allotted Funds	$30,000
Funds Used to Date	$35,314
Funds Remaining	($5,314)

Funds Used to Date: $35,314.00...

Get a copy of this form at: https://www.pattyporto.com/ebooks

LIST OF EXPENSES

Item	Category	Amount
PROJECT FUNDS ALLOTTED $30,000.00	**FUNDS USED TO DATE** $35,314.00	**FUNDS REMAINING** ($5,314.00)
Flooring	Materials max 1pr sq. ft total area 1750 + bathroom floors 371sqft + shower tile & decorative mosaic	$2,550.00
Drywall/Insulation/Tape/Float	Labor	$5,600.00
Drywall	Materials	$1,700.00
Kitchen Cabinets	Materials	$2,600.00
Countertops	Materials/labor	$4,000.00
Base Boards	Materials 0.73 LFT	$1,100.00
Interior Doors	Materials/ 7 x 59.00	$413.00
Appliances	Materials/ Frigidaire Fridge, Stove, Microwave & Dishwasher bundle	$3,000.00
Water Heater	Materials/labor	$600.00
Tile Installation materials	Materials	$520.00
Shower Door	Materials	$400.00
Paint	Materials/labor	$5,000.00
Cabinets install	Labor	$600.00
Flooring	Labor 1.75pr sqft 2121sqft	$2,821.00
Plumbing gen	Labor	$500.00
Electrical Fixtures (face plates, light switches, etc.)	Labor	$1,500.00
Closet Doors	5x39.00	$195.00
Bathrooms	1000x2 All Labor	$2,000.00
Toilets	materials	$215.00
Total		$35,314.00

Category

- 1000x2 All L...
- 5x39.00
- Labor
- Labor 1.75pr ...
- Materials
- Materials 0.7...

If you have drawn a floor plan and 3d models of the reno, send them that as well. There are free programs online you can use to create these, or you can hire someone to do these for you, if you decide to hire someone, include their fee in your scope of work, it is part of your expenses.

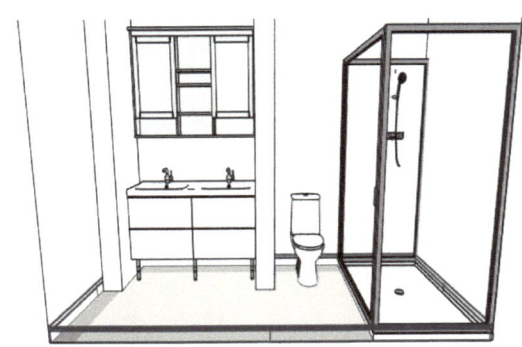

THE REHAB PROCESS

Now let's get to the fun part. The rehab! Who will buy the materials, you or the contractor? There are materials that the contractor can get at discounted prices others not really. Let me let you in on a little secret. You can set up contractor accounts with vendors and get the discounts yourself. Always ad 10% extra material when purchasing just in case.

1. You have now purchased the property and are starting the rehab work. Have your electrical checked AGAIN!! Now that the services are on at that property have your electrician do one more check on ALL outlets and switches. If your design calls for moving or removing walls, the you may need to have both your frame guy and electrician work together. Do not move wall that have electrical outlets without your electrician, do ALL your electrical updating before the drywall goes up. Trust me it is a headache to do it after. Remember that once all walls are up, the property is painted then you will need to install fixtures, lamps, switches, outlets. Make sure this is included in your electrical quote. So, count the lamps, outlets and switches. Some electricians will charge per point (outlet, switch, lamp).

2. Get your plumbing checked and modified before walls go up!! You want to avoid putting holes on the walls, or even water damage when plumbing is being worked on. Do not forget to include your plumbing fixtures in the quote. Count how many sinks, faucets, toilets, dishwashers, tubing, pipes, fittings etc. will need to be installed once the walls, kitchen and bathrooms are done. Major Electrical and Plumbing changes are the first things that need to be worked on.

3. Next is your insulation, what type of insulation will you need. Research the insulation grade and the different types of applications,

sprayed, blown in, rolled, faced, etc. this is important for energy efficiency in the part of the country you are flipping in.

4. Drywall, know the different types of drywall, there sizes, uses etc. YouTube is great to get an idea of how drywall should be installed; I say become a YouTube junkie during this process. Know that wet areas require a different type of drywall than let's say your closet or ceilings. Shower wall will require hardy backer if you are tiling the wall.

5. Tile, what type of tile will you be using? How much does it cost per square foot? What areas of the property will this tile be installed in? what size tile? You researched these prices before you even got that quote, so you have set yourself a budget, don't start making changes now... STAY ON BUDGET. You can design a beautiful bathroom within your budget, just make that budget reasonable from day one.

Here is a sample sheet I created on excel to help me break down the budget for each room and keep track of pricing for each item for my rehab. This is a simple form where I input the description of the item, the store I saw it at, color, style and price. I like to take advantage of online or instore tools to figure out how much of each item I need, many stores will offer tools for free. This spreadsheet is a great tool to keep you within your budget. As I start to list the items I need, I sometimes find that I may have forgotten something or that I'm over my budget. It allows me to add, delete, adjust or change things to accommodate my budget. For example, initially I picked a Vent hood that was $800.00, while working on my list I realized that it was not feasible with my budget so I had to get back to work looking for a nice, economic vent hood that would fit within the design and budget.

KITCHEN   Budget & Check list

ITEM	SIZE	STORE	COLOR	STYLE	QTY	PRICE	TOTAL
Sink Cabinet	36X34.5X24	HD	WHITE	SHAKER	1	158	$ 158.00
Corner Base cabinet							$ -
Base Drawer Cabinet	18x34.5x24	HD	WHITE	SHAKER	2	218	$ 436.00
Corner Wall Cabinet							$ -
Wall Cabinets							$ -
Counter Tops							$ -
Back Splash							$ -
Floor (Tile) (price per box)	13X23	F&D	Bianco	Ceramic	85	19.47	$ 1,654.95
Ceiling							$ -
Elctrical outlets							$ -
Light Fixtures							$ -
Garbage disposal							$ -
Vent Hood wall mounted	30"	Farmhouse kitchen & bath	S/S	WALL MOUNTED	1	319.95	$ 319.95
Door handles for cabinets							$ -
Pantry							$ -
							$ -

TOTAL							$ 2,568.90

Get this template at https://www.pattyporto.com/ebooks

If you are not excel savvy, just write it down. Have your notebook with you and write down your list. Make sure to refer to your list as you purchase items and update pricing if needed.

Notes

WHERE TO SPEND THE MONEY

The kitchen is where your money should be spent most wisely as it can get pricey. Before setting your budget for the kitchen make sure you measure and count how many cabinets you will need, remember there are base and wall cabinets. There are different sizes. Take advantage of free

kitchen design websites and services. Check out the big box stores and the little guys. Have an expert come to the property and measure it for you. Compare their measurements with yours and shop based on that.

Decide what type of countertops you want installed, do not go overboard. Visit properties in the area, what are others putting in their kitchens? Marble, Granite, Formica, Quartz, Concrete, Butcher Block? Compare prices, durability, is it with in your budget? Based on that information use the material that will not just add value to your property but that allows for reasonable comps. What do I

mean by reasonable comps? Well let's say the neighborhood that you are in 90% of the properties have Formica countertops, it doesn't make sense for you to put Quartz in yours, there will be nothing to compare it to, materials that are so out of trend may not give you the value you want. You can change it up a little but don't go overboard. You don't like Formica, well use

the next best material. It is a good idea to stablish a relationship with countertop supply stores, they will usually offer a discount if you have an account with them. I was able to get a 25% discount on the granite for the kitchen and 2 full bathrooms. I paid $1700.00 after the discount was applied. The kitchen had a 108x42" Island, 9ft counter, and 2 4ft long additional counters, a 76" long double sink in the master and 2 46" vanities in the second bath. We purchased 5 slabs of granite and had material left over.

So, either set up accounts with suppliers or befriend your installer he may have accounts with suppliers and pass the savings on to you.

Another area where your money should be well spent is in the bathrooms. A tiny ugly bathroom can turn off a potential buyer and not add value your property.   When you start working on your design, think functional spaces for your Master and secondary bathrooms. Double sinks, nice big tubs, water saving toilets and storage are big sellers. Colors are also very important in your design. Google can give you a billion ideas for those bathrooms. Take your time and chose the design that fits the budget and will give you the biggest bang for your dollar. Befriend some appraisers, it

never hurts to pick their brain as to what adds value and what is just for kicks and giggles. Ask you realtor what they think of your design idea, will these ideas add value, or will they just be for looks. Depending on the area, should you spend money on heated flooring? Should you add a jacuzzi tub? A separate tub and shower are a must in my market area. What are the musts in yours?

Flooring, are you changing the flooring? Are you in a cold or warm climate? The flooring in the property can make a huge difference. So, chose wisely, research the types of tile, wood, concrete, vinyl etc. Make sure you have a professional install your tile. Poorly installed tile is a total turn off and it can cost you extra money to fix it or having to lower your asking price due to badly installed tile.

When purchasing your flooring keep in mind that if you buy flooring that is on sale, there may not be enough for your project. So, what do you do if you just LOVE it but it's on clearance? Before you lose your mind, find out how much you need? Once you know how much of it you will need then ask the store how much they have, if they have enough to cover the area go ahead and purchase it and add 10% to 15% extra material just in case. Never buy just enough material, especially if it's on sale or clearance. In my most recent project, I purchased tile that was on clearance, I purchased just enough to cover the area I was working on, I could have died when I found out that 2 of the 15 boxes of tile were just BROKEN!!

Unusable broken tile is a pain, thankfully the store still had some of that same tile and they exchanged it for me, and I was able to buy more. But never buy just enough ALWAYS buy 10-15% extra material.

When choosing your fixtures, pick a theme and stick to it. Do not make the mistake of having, brass, bronze, gold etc. all mixed in. For example, don't have some door knobs in brass others in bronze. Keep the style and décor as fluid and cohesive as possible. It is a turn off to have multiple different style fixtures throughout the same property. There is a way to marry different styles without making it look crazy.

Crown molding & baseboards make a huge difference in the look of any room and it doesn't have to be expensive. Research supply stores and set up a contractor account to get discounted prices. I've gotten 9/16 x 5-1/4" baseboards for as low as $.73 per linear foot. And 9/16" x 4-1/4" crown molding for $.54 per linear foot. Compare to the big box stores it was a reasonable saving. I spent $575.00 on both for a home with 1826sq ft

Invest in good paint. You don't have to get designer paint but do invest in quality paint and paint job. Your painter can ruin your property if the paint job is crap. Pick neutral but intentional colors for the property. Always keep in mind that this is not your residence so do not get caught up with choosing paint to your liking, chose paint that the general public may like. Many times, people will buy a property and decide to change the paint colors, so again do not pick paint for your taste.

Your design choices will have great impact on how quickly you can sell your property. Always remember you will not be living in this property so do not design for you. Go over your check list several times, always have 10-15% cushion in your budget for unexpected expenses. Hire professionals to do the work, check references if needed, have all your quotes in writing, stay on top of your deadlines.

Make a list of ALL the possible items you may need for the rehab. Walk the property as many times as you need to make sure you don't miss anything. You can use the form below to check off what you may need, add items as you go if needed.

You can get this spreadsheet a: <u>https://www.pattyporto.com/ebooks</u>

ITEM	QTY	PRICE	TOTAL
Kitchen cabinets			$ -
Bathroom Cabinets			$ -
Door Bell	1	$ 149.00	$ 149.00
Smoke detectors	10	$ 25.00	$ 250.00
Faucets	6	$ 100.00	$ 600.00
Toilets	2	$ 100.00	$ 200.00
Bathtubs	2	$ 350.00	$ 700.00
Sinks	3	$ 75.00	$ 225.00
Kitchen Sink	1	$ 350.00	$ 350.00
PVC Electrical Boxes	50	$ 0.39	$ 19.50
Water Heater	1	$ 600.00	$ 600.00
A/C Thermostat	1	$ 100.00	$ 100.00
Electrical Wires			$ -
Electrical outlets			$ -
Light Switches			$ -
GFCI outlets			$ -
Wall Plates			$ -
Drains & Pipes			$ -
Light switches			$ -
Ceiling Fans			$ -
Light Fixtures			$ -
Outdoor lighting			$ -
Plumbing valves			$ -
bathroom exhaust fan			$ -
Vent Hood	1	$ 350.00	$ 350.00
Door Knobs			$ -
Cabinet Door handles			$ -
Insulation			$ -
Drywall	130	$ 7.87	$ 1,023.10
Hardy Backer	20	$ 12.50	$ 250.00
Drywall screws			$ -
Interior Doors			$ -
Outside Doors			$ -
		TOTAL	$ 4,816.60

In the next couple of pages, I have included a few pictures of my latest project. Everything I have shared with you in this book are personal experiences. I am sure there is a lot more to learn about flips as each is different, each property has different needs but if we get organized from day one, we can avoid many obstacles.

My fist flip was a property I found that had been gutted down to the 2x4s. 70% of the frame was rotted, electrical fixtures outdated or gone, floor was covered in dirt left behind by the high waters. The initial quote from the contractor we were working with was $15,000.00, so we figured lets budget for $20,000.00 and get this fantastic deal done and moved forward with making an offer and we closed on the property. It took 3 months to close due to title issues on the seller's side. The deal closed and the work began, about 3 weeks in, we found out that the contractor had no clue what he was doing and underbid the job by about $10,000.00. Now what? Well we are in it we must make it work. We went thru several "contractors" that promised results, took moneys upfront and half assed the job. So, I found myself hiring other people to correct and finish what others had started and doing some of the work myself to save money. In the end we spent a total of $28,000.00 in the rehab. That 28k includes the 15,000.00 the lender financed plus 13,000.00 out of pocket. Here is what our profit looks like, the ARV per the appraisal is $185,000.00 - loan amount $124,500.00+ acquisition cash to close $12,500.00 + out of pocket rehab expenses $13,000.00, Real estate commission for sale $5,550.00+ sale closing cost $5,500.00, +monthly mortgage payments $5,784.00= $18,166.00. So, it wasn't a total loss, but we could have saved a lot of money and time if someone had shared these experiences and tips with us beforehand.

I have included a sample contractor agreement at the end of the book, you can use that and modify to fit your needs. I will also share links to my excel sheets for you to download and use.

The Exit Strategy

What is your plan to flip the property? Will you list it with a real estate company or attempt to sell it yourself? These are important questions to ask yourself as this is the way you will pull the money out of your investment. So, let's talk about listing it with a real estate company, in my opinion is by far the easiest way to sell your property. You can do a traditional listing agreement or try a Flat fee listing.

Traditionally real estate broker will charge 6% commission which covers both the agent that represents you and the buyer's agents commission, they place the property on MLS, and perhaps holds open houses, processes contracts for you and manages showings etc. Ask questions before you sign that listing agreement If you don't feel comfortable with contracts, please let the professionals handle it. I am a former Realtor, so I am very familiar with the process and feel very comfortable handling contract negotiations. You can try selling it yourself but remember that putting a sign on the yard does not guaranty traffic. I personally use the Flat fee listing service. My property appears on MLS, with a full description and photos, gets exposure, and I only pay the buyers agent's commission.

Be very clear as to the details of your property and disclose relevant information. You can limit the types of financing you are willing to accept from the buyer. For example, if you purchase your property under your LLC, you will need to hold tile (in Texas) for at least 91 days before you can accept a contract form a buyer using an FHA loan. Check guidelines in your state before you list your property.

I prefer cash, conventional loans and owner financing. If you decide to offer owner finance, you will want to refinance out of that hard money loan first and make sure your lender doesn't have restrictions on wrapping or owner financing the property to a third party. You want to make sure that you are making payment to that principle. Let your agent know the terms of the owner financing, remember with owner financing you become the lender, so set your interests rate to make sense, set minimum down payment requirements and do your due diligence to make sure the buyer has the ability to repay the debt, foreclosures are a pain.

Another option is refinancing, cashing out and holding the property for rental income. That is a great option if the market is a little slow or if you need to access funds fast to move on to your next project. As promised below are pictures of one of my properties.

Notes

Here is the Sample contractor agreement you can use with your contractors. Always have a written agreement with detailed scope of work attached. You don't have to use this template, find one that fits your needs but ALWAYS have a written contract.

Independent Contractor Agreement for Construction Contractor

This Agreement is made between_____("Client"), with a principal place of business at_____, and _____("Contractor"), with a principal place of business at_____.

1. Services to Be Performed

Contractor will furnish all labor and materials to construct and complete the project shown on the contract documents contained or specified in Exhibit A, which is attached to and made part of this Agreement.

2. Payment

[Choose Alternative A or B.]

[] ALTERNATIVE A

Owner will pay Contractor for all labor and materials the sum of $_____.

[] ALTERNATIVE B

Owner will pay Contractor $_____for labor. Materials will be paid for by Owner upon delivery to the worksite or as follows:

_____

3. Terms of Payment

[Choose Alternative A, B, or C.]

[] ALTERNATIVE A

Upon completing Contractor's services under this Agreement, Contractor will submit an invoice. Owner will pay Contractor within _____days from the date of Contractor's invoice.

[] ALTERNATIVE B

Contractor will be paid $_____upon signing this Agreement and the remaining amount due when Contractor completes the services and submits an invoice. Owner will pay Contractor within_____days from the date of Contractor's invoice.

[] ALTERNATIVE C

Contractor will be paid according to the schedule of payments set forth in Exhibit____, attached to and made part of this Agreement.

4. Time of Completion

The work to be performed under this Agreement will commence on and be substantially completed on or before _____. Time is of the essence.

5. What Constitutes Completion

The work specified in Clause 1 will be considered completed upon approval by Owner; however, Owner's approval will not be unreasonably withheld.

6. Permits and Approvals

[Choose Alternative A or B.]

[] ALTERNATIVE A

Owner will be responsible for determining which state and local permits are necessary for performing the specified work and for obtaining and paying for the permits.

[] ALTERNATIVE B

Contractor will be responsible for determining which state and local permits are necessary for performing the specified work and for obtaining and paying for the permits.

7. Warranty

Contractor warrants that all work will be completed in a good workmanlike manner and in compliance with all building codes and other applicable laws. Contractor agrees to correct any defective work at no cost to Owner. This warranty will be in effect for one year from the date of completion of the work.

8. Liens and Lien Waivers

Contractor represents and warrants that there will be no liens for labor or materials or appliances against the work covered by this Agreement and agrees to protect and hold Owner free and harmless from and against any and all liens and claims for labor, materials, services, or appliances furnished or used in connection with the work.

To protect Owner against liens being filed by Contractor, subcontractors, and materials providers, Contractor agrees that final payment to Contractor under Clause 3 will be withheld by Owner until Contractor presents Owner with lien waivers, lien releases, or acknowledgment of full payment from each subcontractor and materials supplier.

9. Site Maintenance

Contractor agrees to be bound by the following conditions when performing the specified work:

- Contractor will remove all debris and leave the premises in broom-clean condition.

- Contractor will perform the specified work during the following hours:_____.

- Contractor agrees that disruptively loud activities will be performed only at the following times:_____.

- At the end of each day's work, Contractor's equipment will be stored in the following location: _____.

10. Subcontractors

Contractor may at its discretion engage subcontractors to perform services under this Agreement, but Contractor will remain responsible for proper completion of this Agreement.

11. Independent Contractor Status

Contractor is an independent contractor, not Owner's employee. Contractor's employees or subcontractors are not Owner's employees. Contractor and Owner agree to the following rights consistent with an independent contractor relationship.

[Check all that apply.]

[] Contractor has the right to perform services for others during the term of this Agreement.

[] Contractor has the sole right to control and direct the means, manner, and method by which the services required by this Agreement will be performed.

[] Contractor or Contractor's employees or subcontractors will perform the services required by this Agreement; Owner will not hire, supervise, or pay any assistants to help Contractor.

[] Owner will not require Contractor or Contractor's employees or subcontractors to devote full time to performing the services required by this Agreement.

[] Neither Contractor nor Contractor's employees or subcontractors are eligible to participate in any employee pension, health, vacation pay, sick pay, or other fringe benefit plan of Owner.

12. Business Permits, Certificates and Licenses

Contractor represents and warrants that Contractor has complied with all federal, state, and local laws requiring business permits, certificates, and licenses required to carry out the services to be performed under this Agreement.

Contractor's license or registration is for the following type of work and carries the following number:_____.

13. State and Federal Taxes

Client will not:

- withhold FICA (Social Security and Medicare taxes) from Contractor's payments or make FICA payments on Contractor's behalf

- make state or federal unemployment compensation contributions on Contractor's behalf, or

- withhold state or federal income tax from Contractor's payments.

Contractor will pay all taxes incurred while performing services under this Agreement--including all applicable income taxes and, if Contractor is not a corporation, self-employment (Social Security) taxes. Upon demand, Contractor will provide Client with proof that such payments have been made.

14. Fringe Benefits

Contractor understands that neither Contractor nor Contractor's employees or subcontractors are eligible to participate in any employee pension, health, vacation pay, sick pay, or other fringe benefit plan of Client. If Contractor is subsequently classified by the IRS as a common law employee, Contractor expressly waives his or her rights to any benefits to which he or she was, or might have become, entitled.

15. Workers' Compensation

Client will not obtain workers' compensation insurance on behalf of Contractor or Contractor's employees or subcontractors. Contractor will provide Contractor's employees and subcontractors with workers' compensation insurance to the extent required by law and provide Client with a certificate of workers' compensation insurance.

[Optional: Check if applicable.]

[] Contractor will obtain workers' compensation insurance coverage for Contractor. Contractor will provide Client with proof that such coverage has been obtained before starting work. *[End option.]*

16. Unemployment Compensation

Client will make no state or federal unemployment compensation payments on behalf of Contractor or Contractor's employees or contract personnel. Contractor will not be entitled to these benefits in connection with work performed under this Agreement.

17. Insurance

Client will not provide any insurance coverage of any kind for Contractor or Contractor's employees or subcontractors. Contractor will maintain a broad form commercial general liability insurance policy providing combined single limits of not less than $_____ per occurrence and $_____annual aggregate. Before commencing any work, Contractor will provide Client with proof of this insurance and that Client has been made an additional insured under the policy.

Contractor will indemnify and hold Client harmless from any loss or liability arising from performing services under this Agreement.

18. Terminating the Agreement

[Choose Alternative A or B.]

[] ALTERNATIVE A

With reasonable cause, either Client or Contractor may terminate this Agreement, effective immediately upon giving written notice.

Reasonable cause includes:

- a material violation of this Agreement, or

- any act exposing the other party to liability to others for personal injury or property damage.

[] ALTERNATIVE B

Either party may terminate this Agreement any time by giving_____days' written notice to the other party of the intent to terminate.

19. Exclusive Agreement

This Agreement (including any attached exhibits) is the entire Agreement between Contractor and Client.

[Optional Clause: Check box if applicable.]

[] 20. Modifying the Agreement

This Agreement may be modified only by a writing signed by both parties.

[End Optional Clause]

21. Resolving Disputes

/[] ALTERNATIVE A

If a dispute arises under this Agreement, any party may take the matter to court.

[Optional: Check if applicable.]

[] If any court action is necessary to enforce this Agreement, the prevailing party will be entitled to reasonable attorney fees, costs, and expenses in addition to any other relief to which the party may be entitled. *[End Option.]*

[] ALTERNATIVE B

If a dispute arises under this Agreement, the parties agree to first try to resolve the dispute with the help of a mutually agreed-upon mediator in ___ *[list city or county where mediation will occur]* ___. Any costs and fees other than attorney fees associated with the mediation will be shared equally by the parties. If the dispute is not resolved within 30 days after it is referred to the mediator, any party may take the matter to court.

[Optional: Check if applicable.]

[] If any court action is necessary to enforce this Agreement, the prevailing party will be entitled to reasonable attorney fees, costs, and expenses in addition to any other relief to which the party may be entitled.

[] ALTERNATIVE C

Choose Alternative A, B, or C and any desired optional clauses.]

If a dispute arises under this Agreement, the parties agree to first try to resolve the dispute with the help of a mutually agreed-upon mediator in___ *[list city or county where mediation will occur]* ___. Any costs and fees other than attorney fees associated with the mediation will be shared equally by the parties. If it proves impossible to arrive at a mutually satisfactory solution through mediation, the parties agree to submit the dispute to a mutually agreed-upon arbitrator in___ *[list city or county where arbitration will occur]* ___. Judgment upon the award rendered by the arbitrator may be entered in any court having jurisdiction to do so. Costs of arbitration, including attorney fees, will be allocated by the arbitrator.

22. Applicable Law

This Agreement will be governed by the laws of the state of_____.

23. Notices

All notices and other communications in connection with this Agreement will be in writing and will be considered given as follows:

- when delivered personally to the recipient's address as stated on this Agreement

- three days after being deposited in the United States mail, with postage prepaid to the recipient's address as stated on this Agreement, or

- when sent by fax or electronic mail, such notice is effective upon receipt provided that a duplicate copy of the notice is promptly given by first class mail or the recipient delivers a written confirmation of receipt.

24. No Partnership

This Agreement does not create a partnership relationship. Neither party has authority to enter into contracts on the other's behalf.

Signatures

Owner:____ *[Name of Owner]* ____

By: _____Signature

Typed or Printed Name: _____

Title: _____

Date: _____

Contractor: ____ *[Name of Contractor]* ____

By: _____Signature

Typed or Printed Name: _____

Title: _____

Taxpayer ID Number: _____

Date: _____

You can get this sample contract at https://www.pattyporto.com/ebooks

      I hope the information I provided is useful to you. I'd love to hear how your 1st flip went, please share with me any questions, ideas or testimonial you may have. I'm here to serve and it is my goal to help you be successful. For one on one consulting visit my page at www.pattyporto.com or email me at patty@pattyporto.com